MW00622922

Hey Kids! Let's Visit San Diego

Fun, Facts, and Amazing Discoveries for Kids

Teresa Mills

Life Experiences Publishing

Contents

Welcome   1

A Little About San Diego   3

1. USS Midway Museum   9

2. Maritime Museum of San Diego   13

3. Balboa Park   17

4. San Diego Zoo   25

5. Fleet Science Center   29

6. San Diego Natural History Museum   33

7. San Diego Air and Space Museum   37

8. Old Town San Diego State Historic Park   41

9. Little Italy   45

10. The New Children's Museum   47

11. Seaport Village   49

12. San Diego-Coronado Bridge   53

13. Unconditional Surrender Statue   57

14. Belmont Park   61

15. SeaWorld San Diego   65

16. La Jolla Cove   69

17. Birch Aquarium at Scripps   73

18. Torrey Pines State Natural Reserve   77

19. San Diego Zoo Safari Park   81

20. San Diego Botanic Garden   85

21. The Carlsbad Flower Fields   89

22. Cabrillo National Monument   91

23. Whale Watching in San Diego   99

24. Walking Tours   103

25. Bike and Kayak Tours   105

Welcome

San Diego is located on the west coast of the United States. It is a city full of things to do and see including a zoo, parks, museums, and the beach. San Diego is sometimes referred to as the birthplace of California because this was the first site that was settled on the west coast of the United States.

This book is written as a fun fact guide about some attractions and sites in San Diego. It includes some history interspersed with fun facts about things to do. The book can easily be enjoyed by younger children through reading it with them. You can visit San Diego right from your own home! Whether you are preparing for a vacation with the family and want to learn more about the city or just want to learn a little more about the birthplace of California, this book is for you.

As you continue to learn more about San Diego, I have some fun activity and coloring pages that you can download and print at:

https://kid-friendly-family-vacations.com/sdfun

When you have completed this book, I invite you to visit the other cities in the series:

Hey Kids! Let's Visit Washington DC
Hey Kids! Let's Visit A Cruise Ship
Hey Kids! Let's Visit New York City
Hey Kids! Let's Visit London England
Hey Kids! Let's Visit San Francisco
Hey Kids! Let's Visit Savannah Georgia
Hey Kids! Let's Visit Paris France
Hey Kids! Let's Visit Charleston South Carolina
Hey Kids! Let's Visit Chicago
Hey Kids! Let's Visit Rome Italy
Hey Kids! Let's Visit Boston
Hey Kids! Let's Visit Philadelphia
Hey Kids! Let's Visit San Diego
Hey Kids! Let's Visit Seattle
Hey Kids! Let's Visit Seoul South Korea

Enjoy!

Teresa Mills

A Little About San Diego

San Diego is a city in southern California set along the Pacific Ocean. It is protected from the Pacific Ocean by two peninsulas, Point Loma and the Coronado / Silver Strand peninsula, which help form the San Diego Bay. San Diego is one of the most populated cities in the United States with a city population of close to 1.3 million, and it is the second largest city in California (Los Angeles is number 1). A couple of things that San Diego is famous for are its 70 miles of beaches and mild temperatures year-round.

In addition to all the things to do in the city of San Diego, there are places to see and visit both to the north and south of the city. Some places away from the city that we will explore are the Torrey Pines State Natural Preserve, the Birch Aquarium, the San Diego Zoo Safari Park, and Cabrillo National Monument.

Juan Rodriguez Cabrillo landed in the San Diego Bay in 1542 and claimed the area for Spain. This was 200 years before any other Europeans would live in the area. Before the Europeans, though, Native Americans such as the Kumeyaay were San Diego's first residents.

A fort and a mission were built in 1769, which became the first settlement under Spanish and then Mexican rule. San Diego became a part of the United States in 1848 and was given the honor of being the county seat of San Diego County when California became a state in 1850.

Today, and since World War II, the military has played a large role in the local economy of San Diego. The major industry in San Diego today is military and defense, with over 40,000 people employed at the San Diego Naval Base. San Diego is also home to the University of California San Diego, one of the top-rated public universities in the United States.

Ready? Let's Visit San Diego!

Old Town San Diego State Historic Park

Balboa Park

Little Italy

Maritime Museum

Unconditional Surrender Statue

USS Midway Museum

Fleet Science Center

Air & Space Museum

Natural History Museum

The New Children's Museum

Seaport Village

Coronado Bridge

Cabrillo National Monument

Map of San Diego Attractions

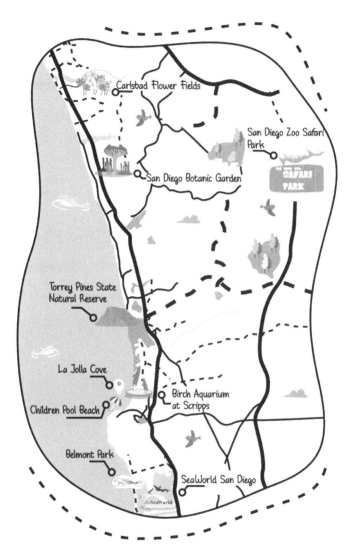

Map of Attractions North of San Diego

Chapter 1

USS Midway Museum

The USS Midway Museum is a museum dedicated to the historical USS Midway Aircraft Carrier. The museum is located in downtown San Diego at 910 North Harbor Drive. As a part of the museum, you will see a large collection of aircrafts – some that were built in southern California.

Opened to the public on June 7, 2004, the annual visits to the museum increased yearly and by 2015 it was the most popular naval warship museum in the U.S. While visiting the museum, you can see many places inside the carrier on the self-guided audio tour including the galley, the bridge, the post office, the brig, the engine room, the officers' quarters, and the primary flight control. The museum also includes many climb-aboard aircraft.

The flight deck of the USS Midway is 1,001 feet (305 meters) long with an area of 4 acres (1.6 hectares). That is large enough for more than two American football fields to be placed end-to-end on the flight deck.

USS Midway Flight Deck

The USS Midway served the U.S. Navy for 47 years from 1945-1992 and was the only aircraft carrier to serve the entire Cold War (a time of geopolitical unrest between the U.S. and the Soviet Union and their allies with no large-scale fighting) and beyond. That is the longest that an aircraft carrier served in the 20th century. During those 47 years of active service, the USS Midway was home to more than 200,000 sailors.

USS Midway

Fun Facts About the USS Midway and Museum

- *Top Gun: Maverick* star Tom Cruise appeared on the flight deck of the USS Midway during Paramount Pictures' "Top Gun: Maverick Global Premier Red Carpet Fan Experience." San Diego was the setting of the *Top Gun* movies.

- The USS Midway offers a program that allows kids to sleep over on the carrier. The program is called Snooze Crewz. Kids who participate get to sleep in the crew berths aboard the aircraft carrier.

- The Battle of Midway was one of the most important naval battles of World War II. Onboard the USS Midway, there is a 90-seat theater that shows the 15-minute film "Voices of Midway," a film that tells the story of the battle through the voices of men who took part in the battle.

Chapter 2

Maritime Museum of San Diego

Just down the street from the USS Midway at 1492 North Harbor Drive is the Maritime Museum of San Diego. Here you will find one of the largest number of historic ships and other vessels in same place in all of the U.S. The self-guided walking tour of the museum allows you to explore this historic fleet.

The main attraction at the museum is the Star of India, a merchant ship from 1863. The Star of India is the oldest ship still sailing regularly, and she is the oldest iron-hulled merchant ship still floating today. Originally named the Euterpe, she was a full-rigged ship (a ship with three masts, all square rigged, which means driven by a wooden pole that is perpendicular or "square" to the bottom of the ship).

The Star of India

The other ships at the museum include:

- The Californian – The official Tall Ship of California, which was built in the San Diego Bay and launched for the 1984 Olympic Games in Los Angeles.

- The HMS Surprise – This ship started out as a replica of the 18th century Royal Navy frigate named Rose in 1970. She was then transformed into a replica 24-gun frigate for the film *Master and Commander: The Far Side of the World.* The replica, which is now the HMS Surprise, joined the lineup at the museum in 2004.

- San Salvador – This is the ship that brought Juan Rodriguez Cabrillo to San Diego in 1542. She was the first ship to survey the California coast. The ship you see today is a replica of the original San Salvador, built to painstaking specifications by a group of professional boat builders.

- Steam Ferry Berkley – This ferryboat operated on the San Francisco Bay for 60 years. She was built in 1898 and is a California State Historic Landmark as well as a National Historic Landmark.

- Steam Yacht Medea – This yacht was built in 1904 for William Macalister Hall. She is built of steel and furnished with oak and teak. The Medea served in World War II as a Royal Navy barrage balloon vessel (a long flat vessel that normally accompanied merchant ships during wartime and flew a balloon to help deter enemy attack). By 1964, it was back in civilian service.

- 555 USS Dolphin – This submarine has the distinction of being the deepest diving sub in the world.

- PCF 816 Swift Boat – PCF stands for Patrol Craft Fast as they were named by the U.S. Navy. The men aboard just called them Swift Boats.

- San Diego Harbor Pilot Boat – This 1914 pilot boat served as San Diego's chief pilot craft until 1996. Pilot ships would greet incoming merchant ships and guide them into port.

Fun Facts About the Maritime Museum of San Diego

- The ship, the Californian, hosts in overnight Living History programs. These programs are for students, but a few times each year, they are opened to the public.

- The Steam Yacht Medea was constructed in only 51 days – a record time!

- The Steam Ferry Berkley worked night and day rescuing victims of the 1906 earthquake in San Francisco.

Chapter 3

Balboa Park

Balboa Park is a 1,200-acre (485.62-hectares) urban park just northwest of downtown San Diego. It is lovingly called San Diego's 1,200-acre backyard. Plans for the park started in 1892 when the city set aside 1,400 acres (566.56 hectares) of land, then the land sat without formal development for over 20 years. Starting in 1892, Kate Sessions, a commercial nursery owner, made some contributions to the park. Ms. Sessions agreed to plant 100 trees per year in the park as well as provide shrubs and trees other places in the city in exchange for 32 acres of land to use for her business. Kate Sessions was given the title "The Mother of Balboa Park" during the 1935 California Pacific International Exposition.

The park hosted two major California Expositions – the Panama-California Exposition in 1915-1916 and the California Pacific International Exposition in 1935-1936. Before the Panama-California Exposition in 1915, the park was still called "City Park." City leaders of San

Diego decided that a better name was needed as preparations were being made to host the exposition. So, in 1910 Park Commissioners looked at various name suggestions (Silver Gate Park, San Diego Park, Horton Park, and Miramar Park) settling on Balboa Park in honor of Vasco Nunez de Balboa – the first European to spot the Pacific Ocean while exploring in Panama.

Balboa Park has open spaces, walking trails, museums, theaters, and even the San Diego Zoo. Walking along the El Prado (the main thoroughfare of the park), you will see other walkers, bikers, tourists, and some of San Diego's grandest buildings. Many of these buildings were constructed for the Panama-California Exposition but are still around today. The picture below is of the Casa del Prado, now a theater in Balboa Park.

Casa del Prado on El Prado

Beautiful Spanish architecture will surround you as you stroll down El Prado. Along the way is another great historic landmark – the California Tower. Inside the California Tower you will find the San Diego Museum of Us.

The park has 18 museums:

- Centro Cultural de la Raza – A cultural arts center raising awareness of the Chicano, Mexico Latino, and Indigenous culture.

- Comic-Con Museum – A shrine for everything comic book related.

- Fleet Science Center – Investigate and explore the wonders of science and innovation.

- Japanese Friendship Garden of San Diego – Celebrate the connection between San Diego and its sister city of Yokohama, Japan.

- The Marston House – Built in 1905 by the "Father of Balboa Park" George M. Marston, this home is situated on 5 acres (2 hectares) of gardens.

- Mingei International Museum – a museum dedicated to folk art.

- Museum of Photographic Arts – a museum dedicated to photography.

The California Tower in Balboa Park

- San Diego Air & Space Museum – an affiliate of the Smithsonian Institution, this air and space museum is home to a collection illustrating the history of flight.

- Institute of Contemporary Art San Diego – an art museum highlighting works by San Diego artists.

- San Diego Automotive Museum – an automotive museum featuring many unique vehicles of the 20th century.

- San Diego History Center – dedicated to the heritage of the San Diego region.

- San Diego Model Railroad Museum – the world's largest model railroad museum. In the museum, you will find four large model layouts of Southwest railroads.

- San Diego Museum of Us – This museum is in the historic California Tower. The museum offers exhibits covering a large range of human history and culture.

- San Diego Natural History Museum – This museum explores the history from past to present of southern California.

- The San Diego Museum of Art – art collections of Spanish and Italian old masters. The museum features rotating exhibits from around the world as well as educational and cultural programs.

- Timken Museum of Art – This museum is known as San Diego's "jewel box" of fine art because of the paintings by world-renowned European Old Masters. There are paintings by Bruegel, Hals, and Rembrandt in the museum.

- Veterans Museum & Memorial Center – honors those who served. The museum offers the history of the Air Force, the Army, the Marines, the Coast Guard, and the Merchant Marines.

- WorldBeat Center – a museum dedicated to preserve and promote African and African American cultures.

In addition to the museums, Balboa Park also has 17 different gardens that create a botanical oasis in San Diego. The list of attractions and venues range from the San Diego Zoo to Balboa Stadium (which was home to the San Diego Chargers until 1996 and is now used by the San Diego High School) to the Morley Field Sports Complex (disc golf, a dog park, bocce ball courts, an archery range, and more). It seems that there is just no end to the things available to do in Balboa Park.

Balboa Park Fountain

Fun Facts About Balboa Park

- Balboa Park is larger than Central Park in New York City. Central Park is 842 acres (340.75 hectare).

- The park most likely would not have existed without the creation of the Panama Canal. The canal was completed in 1914 and once the Atlantic and Pacific were connected, San Diego was the first port of call on the Pacific Coast of the U.S. This created the opportunity for San Diego to host the Panama-California Exposition in 1915 in Balboa Park.

- Both the Beatles and the Rolling Stones played in Balboa Park early in their musical careers.

Chapter 4

San Diego Zoo

The San Diego Zoo is a part of Balboa Park and is home to a huge number of animals – close to 12,000. There are over 650 species and subspecies of animals. It is also an accredited botanical garden with more than 700,000 plants. The zoo grew out of the Panama-California Exposition exotic animal exhibits that were abandoned. This led to the creation of the Zoological Society of San Diego in 1916.

This large zoo is set on 100 acres (40.47 hectares) within Balboa Park. The zoo offers a guided tour bus that covers almost 75% of the park, so that's a cool way to get an overview of all the things to do and see. An app is also available to make your trip easier, and it is GPS-enabled so you can see where you are within the park at any point in time.

Flamingos at the San Diego Zoo

As you visit the zoo in San Diego, spend time looking at each animal habitat and learning a little more about them. There are so many to see.

Sea Seal at the San Diego Zoo

Fun Facts About the San Diego Zoo

- The San Diego Zoo was a pioneer among zoos in creating cageless, open air, more natural habitats for the animals.

- The San Diego Zoo was created to provide a permanent home for the animals brought in for the 1915 Panama-California Exposition.

- There is a tram in the zoo that gives visitors an aerial view of the entire park. The tram is known as the Skyfari and was built in 1969.

Chapter 5

Fleet Science Center

The Fleet Science Center is also located in Balboa Park. It is a planetarium and science museum that was named for aviation pioneer Reuben H. Fleet. Fleet helped found the U.S. Air Mail Service as well as operating a business in San Diego called Consolidated Aircraft. The Fleet Family made the initial gift that helped establish this science center.

Some of the things that you will find to do at the Fleet Science Center are:

- Watch a film in the first IMAX Dome Theater in the world, the Heikoff Giant Dome Theater. Film presentations are shown here daily, and there is a monthly astronomer-led planetarium show called "The Sky Tonight."

- Learn about video game development in the *Design Zone*.

- Confuse your brain in the *Illusions* (optical illusions) exhibit.

- Become a "human battery" in *It's Electric*!

- Learn about nano technology (technology so small you can't see it) in *Nano*.

- Learn about the San Diego power grid in *Power Play San Diego*.

- Check out the sources of San Diego's water supply in *San Diego's Water*.

- Generate your own electricity in the energy exhibit *So Watt!*

- Explore the universe like NASA and learn about the solar system and beyond in *Sun, Earth, Universe*.

Fun Facts About the Fleet Science Center

- The Fleet Science Center was the first science center that combined interactive science displays with a large screen IMAX theater and a planetarium. This design set the pattern for other large science museums.

- There are a lot of rotating exhibits at the science center, so you never really know what you might find that's exciting to do.

- The science center has a variety of science clubs for kids. Check out the schedule, you may be able to join in on one.

Chapter 6

San Diego Natural History Museum

The Nat – or the San Diego Natural History Museum – is located in Balboa Park. Founded in 1874, it was originally called the San Diego Society of Natural History. The current home of the museum opened in 1933 and an expansion in 2001 doubled the museum space.

The San Diego Society of Natural History was started by a group of amateur naturalists. They wanted to be a go-to source for scientific culture. They wanted to serve members of the community who wanted to learn and make contributions to the scientific study in the San Diego area. The society has been doing just that ever since.

The group was a great protector of the Torrey Pines State Natural Reserve. From 1883, they started encouraging the city and county to start a preservation society to protect the Torrey pine. In the mid-1920s, the Torrey Pines Reserve was formed.

The Society of Natural History opened its first museum in the summer of 1912. The museum was in a single room of the Hotel Cecil in downtown San Diego. The first exhibits came from the collections of Frank and Kate Stephens. Ever growing, the museum was later housed in three different buildings in Balboa Park from 1917-1933. Their permanent home on El Prado in Balboa Park was dedicated on January 14, 1933.

The San Diego Natural History Museum

Some cool things to see and do in the museum are:

- Living Lab – brings you eye to eye with rarely seen, not so cuddly animals of the San Diego region. In the Living Lab, you will see animals that sting, crawl, and climb. You might see a rattlesnake, frogs, arachnids, centipedes, or a Gila monster.

- Hidden Gems – You will see more than 100 bright, spectacular gems and minerals. The San Diego area is full of these gems and minerals; it is one of the most well-known gem-producing areas in the world.

- Fossil Mysteries – mastodons, dinosaurs, and other fossil history of the San Diego area.

- Coast to Cactus in Southern California – San Diego is an interesting area to explore, and this exhibit explores the differing terrains that can be found in the region – beaches, mountains, and deserts.

- Extraordinary Ideas from Ordinary People: A History of Citizen Science – This exhibit shines a light on naturalists from the past and the present. You will see rare books, photos, artwork, and documents along with touchable experiences to learn more about the displays.

- Demonstration Lab – a window into the world of working scientists.

- The Backyard – a unique hands-on play place for young explorers.

- Skulls – Skulls, skulls, everywhere! Over 200 skulls are on display from birds, mammals, reptiles, and amphibians.

Fun Facts About the San Diego Natural History Museum

- There is an Allosaurus skeleton in the main lobby of the museum. The skeleton is lovingly called Alice, or "Al."

- Look for Meg, a megalodon (the Giant "Mega-Tooth" shark). She is suspended from the ceiling of the atrium.

- Try out a scavenger hunt while visiting the *Fossil Mysteries* section of the museum.

Chapter 7

San Diego Air and Space Museum

The San Diego Air and Space Museum is located in Balboa Park. The museum is an affiliate of the Smithsonian Institution and has a variety of aviation history artifacts on display.

San Diego has a big history in the aviation world. Convair, the company that built the B-25 Liberator and the PBY Catalina, was founded in San Diego.

The Air and Space Museum was established in San Diego in 1961 and opened its doors on February 15, 1963, in the old Food and Beverage building in Balboa Park. The museum was an immediate success. By 1965, the museum needed more space, so it was moved to the Electric Building close by. Plans were being made in the 1970s to move the museum to the Ford Building (a historic building in Balboa Park that had been put on the National Register of Historic Places in 1973). Before the museum could be moved to the Ford Building, there was a fire in the Electric Building in 1978. Fifty or more aircraft were completely lost in the fire.

The City of San Diego started an Aerospace Museum recovery fund to help raise funds to rebuild. The new Air and Space Museum opened in the Ford Building on February 22, 1980.

The galleries to see at the Air and Space Museum are:

- World War I Gallery – Here you will learn about some of the fighter "aces" of WWI – The Red Baron, Billy Bishop, and Eddie Rickenbacker.

- World War II Gallery – Airplanes were being produced at a great rate in the United States during World War II. Some of the aircraft on display are the Spitfire and the Japanese Zero.

- Theodore Gildred Rotunda – Mr. Gildred was a San Diego resident who embarked on a 19-day, 4200-mile (6760-km) goodwill flight to South America. Later, his son recreated this flight. The rotunda honors the aviation history of San Diego.

- Modern Jet & Space Age Gallery - dedicated to Wally Schirra, who flew in all three early space programs (Mercury, Gemini, and Apollo).

- Golden Age of Flight Gallery – dedicated to flight in the years 1919-1939. This was a time of peace and a maturing of the air programs in the U.S.

- Edwin D. McKellar Pavilion of Flight – the center of the museum where most special programs are held.

Fun Facts About the San Diego Air and Space Museum

- The museum has a 3D/4D theater. It shows different movies in each format.

- There are flight simulators in the museum where you can experience taking off and flying a fighter plane.

- The original Apollo 9 command module is on display at the museum.

Chapter 8

Old Town San Diego State Historic Park

Old Town San Diego State Historic Park is located just north of San Diego at 2829 Juan Street. This park allows visitors a chance to explore the history of San Diego by taking a look at the past. The State Historic Park was established in 1968 and is a living history museum. It has preserved many historic buildings dating back to the 19th century, showing San Diego's early history from 1820-1870.

Old Town San Diego State Historic Park

Some great exhibits at the Old Town San Diego State Historic Park are:

- The Visitor Center – see a diorama of Old Town from the 1892 timeframe. The building itself is historical as it was used as the San Diego Herald offices.

- The McCoy House - a home built originally in 1869 by Sheriff James McCoy for his wife Winifred.

- The Seeley Stable – wagons, buggies, and horse-drawn carriages of the mid-19th century.

- The Colorado House – a successful hotel in its day, built in 1851.

- Wells Fargo Museum – a museum dedicated to banking, mining, and stagecoach travel.

- Mason Street School – the first publicly owned schoolhouse in San Diego County, built in 1865.

Fun Facts About the Old Town San Diego State Historic Park

- The Old Town San Diego State Historic Park is the most visited state park in California according to the historic park's website.

- Old Town San Diego has long been called "the birthplace" of California. San Diego was the homeplace of the first Spanish settlement in California around 1769.

- At the time that California became a state (1850), San Diego was still mostly located in the Old Town area.

Chapter 9

Little Italy

San Diego's Little Italy is one of the oldest areas of the city, and one of the most historical too! It covers just over 48 blocks, so it is one of the largest Little Italy communities in the U.S. When this community was first created, it was a Portuguese and Italian fishing neighborhood.

The neighborhood today is full of Italian restaurants and grocery stores. You will find frequent festivals and even a weekly farmers market. I love walking through a community like this – it gives a good feel of Italian culture and allows you to try real Italian cooking – even if it is pizza.

Little Italy - San Diego

Fun Facts About Little Italy in San Diego

- The trees planted by the sidewalks are planted just about 10 steps apart.

- Walk through Amici Park to see the recipe tables. On the tables are sculptures of dishes of food. Then next to the food sculptures is the recipe on a plaque with raised lettering. Bring paper and pencil, and you can rub a copy of the recipes.

- The Little Italy sign (in the picture above) was built to honor the immigrants who created this neighborhood.

Chapter 10

The New Children's Museum

The New Children's Museum in San Diego is located downtown at 200 W Island Ave. This museum is set up to allow children to move around and strengthen their bodies as they sharpen their minds. The museum is art-based, and it commissions artists to create room-sized playscapes that allow children to explore, play, and interact.

The New Children's Museum's Mission is to spark creativity, exploration, and a sense of belonging through interactive art experiences.

The museum initially opened in 1983 in La Jolla (a seaside community within San Diego) and was called the Children's Museum of San Diego. After 10 years in this location, the museum moved to the downtown San Diego area and became the Children's Museum. Then in 2008, the museum again changed their name to the New Children's Museum to signal that they were now focusing on working with contemporary artists to create their play spaces.

Fun Facts About the New Children's Museum

- During the 2020 Covid pandemic, the museum had to close its doors and furlough employees (ask employees to take a temporary leave from work). Almost right away, the museum created #thinkplaycreatefromhome to help families with online resources for play at home.

- The "Sketch Aquarium" allows kids to create a colorful sea creature and then watch it come to life on the wall sized aquarium.

- There is a room in the museum that is filled with more that 40 mattresses and more than 60 tire pillows – enjoy the simple pleasure of jumping on a bed!

Chapter 11

Seaport Village

San Diego's Seaport Village is built to look like
a classic waterfront village of over a century ago.
Seaport Village opened in 1980 and is a 14-acre
(5.67 hectares) waterfront entertainment, dining, and
shopping complex. There are more than 50 shops and
many casual and fine dining restaurants. The village also
has four miles (6.44 km) of cobblestone paths and a
1/4-mile (0.4-km) boardwalk along the bay.

Seaport Village

The Seaport Village complex is built on land that is over Punta de los Muertos (Point of the Dead), where the 1782 Spanish expedition buried those who died from scurvy, which is a disease caused by a lack of vitamin C. Ground was broken for the village in 1978, and the village complex opened two years later.

Fun Facts About Seaport Village

- The village is home to a carousel that dates back to 1895 and features hand carved animals. This carousel was built in Brooklyn, NY, and has been featured at Fair Park in Dallas, TX; Pacific Ocean Park in Santa Monica, CA; Washington state; Portland Oregon; Burbank, CA; and finally, its home in San Diego.

- Keep your eyes peeled at Christmastime, and you might just see Surfin' Santa at the village.

- You can hop onto a San Diego SEAL Tour from Seaport Village. The tour is taken on an amphibious vehicle, meaning that it can drive around town and launch straight into the water for a harbor tour as well.

Chapter 12

San Diego-Coronado Bridge

The San Diego-Coronado Bridge (or Coronado Bridge) opened for traffic from San Diego to Coronado on August 3, 1969. It is a 2.12-mile (3.41-km) bridge that has a 200-ft (61-m) vertical clearance. This height allows most ships to pass underneath it. The 90-degree curve that you see in the bridge was added to get to the 200 ft (61 m) elevation without being too steep.

The bridge towers (there are thirty of them that the bridge rests upon) are supported by a tall, tapered arch that looks like the Spanish mission church arches. These arches can be seen all around Southern California. Also, the bridge is blue. Caltrans (the California transportation authority) states that the bridge must be re-painted regularly to maintain this color, but it is worth it to keep the color that connects the bridge to the sea.

The San Diego-Coronado Bridge

Fun Facts About the San Diego-Coronado Bridge

- The bridge cuts 17 miles (27.36 km) off the drive from Coronado to San Diego (or San Diego to Coronado). Coronado is on a peninsula that can be reached by land from San Diego, but it is a 19-mile (30.58-km) drive.

- The Coronado Bridge won an architectural design award – the "Most Beautiful Bridge" award from the American Institute of Steel Construction.

- The bridge has five lanes for traffic. The center lane can switch directions by moving a concrete barrier. It is moved by a vehicle that is specially designed to do this, called a road zipper.

Chapter 13

Unconditional Surrender Statue

This giant statue that is located along the San Diego Bay not far from the USS Midway Museum is known by several names: the Kissing Sailor Statue, Embracing Peace, or Unconditional Surrender. The statue is a very large replica of the famous "V-J Day in Times Square" photograph that was snapped on August 14, 1945. World War II was officially over, and this photograph was taken either by photographer Lt. Victor Jorgensen or Albert Eisenstaedt (both took an almost identical photograph) as a sailor grabs the first girl he saw and kisses her.

After the photographs were taken, J. Seward Johnson (a philanthropist and artist) produced versions of the kissing couples using urethane and foam which he called "Unconditional Surrender." What you see today is one of these replicas. It came to San Diego in 2007.

The Unconditional Surrender Statue

Fun Facts About the Unconditional Surrender Statue

- The statue stands 25 ft (7.62 m) tall and weighs in at 6,000 pounds (2,721.6 kg).

- San Diego fell in love with the statue, and when the foam version started wearing down, they decided to buy one in permanent bronze. The $1,000,000 cost was raised by donations to the USS Midway Museum. The new bronze statue was placed in 2013.

- Other replicas of the photograph are on display in Pearl Harbor, HI, and Hamilton, NJ.

Chapter 14

Belmont Park

Belmont Park is a beachfront entertainment and amusement park on Mission Beach in San Diego. The park opened on July 4, 1925, originally as the Mission Beach Amusement Center. The Giant Dipper roller coaster is thought of as a local landmark and is listed on the National Register of Historic Places.

The park development was done by John D. Spreckels, a businessman credited with helping San Diego become a major commercial center. Speculation is that Mr. Spreckels built Belmont Park to help him sell land in the Mission Beach area. The park does attract many visitors each year, so it may have been a spart move on Spreckels' part.

Belmont Park Aerial View

Belmont Park today offers rides (including the historic Giant Dipper), oceanfront restaurants, and other attractions. At the park you can experience:

- The Giant Dipper – A big thrill wooden roller coaster

- Control Freak – A big thrill gyro loop that allows riders to control the drive and clutch action.

- Beach Blaster – A big thrill revolution ride that swings and rotates 360 degrees at the same time.

- Octotron – A big thrill that travels on a roller coaster like track. Riders can control the speed of the spin and forward/backward motion.

- Overgrive Bumper Cars – A little thrill classic bumper car ride.

- Krazy Cars – A little thrill ride with inner tube shaped cars.

- Tilt-A-Whirl – A little thrill classic tilt-a-whirl with ice cream shaped cars.

- Mic Drop – A little thrill and gentler drop tower for children.

- Liberty Carousel – A little thrill classic carousel (merry-go-round) ride.

- Dip N Dive – A little thrill submarine themed ride for kids and a chaperone.

- Wave Jumper – A little thrill ride for kids.

- Speedway – A little thrill racecar themed track for kids to experience driving.

- Zero Gravity – A big thrill drop tower.

- Laser Tag and Laser Maze

- Sky Ropes – A ropes course.

- A rock wall

- A zip line course

- Tiki Town Mini Golf

- Xanadu 7D (real-time 3D graphics and 4D movie) Theater

- Coconut Climb – A rock climbing experience where you climb coconut trees.

- An arcade and midway games

- Escapology San Diego

- Belmont Lanes bowling

- An old-time photo booth

The rides and attractions will keep anyone busy for a long, long time! In addition to all of that, there are sit-down beachfront restaurants and places to grab a quick bite to eat – from pizza and tacos to burgers and hot dogs to sweets!

Fun Facts About Belmont Park

- The Giant Dipper roller coaster originally opened in 1925.

- The Monster Waffle Cone at the Sweet Shop is not to be missed!

- The Dole Whip that was made famous at Disney and in Hawaii is served in Belmont Park.

Chapter 15

SeaWorld San Diego

SeaWorld is an animal-themed amusement park located on Mission Bay in San Diego. SeaWorld has three locations currently – Orlando, Florida, San Antonia Texas, and San Diego, California! The park offers animal experiences as well as rides and other attractions.

SeaWorld is always a great option for a way to spend the day. The park is laid out over 100 acres (40.5 hectares) on Mission Bay and has educational presentations with animals along with seasonal events.

Orca Encounter at SeaWorld San Diego

The animals at the park that you may have an opportunity to see include tropical birds, eels, dolphins, penguins, sea lions, orcas, belugas, otters, flamingos, sharks, sea turtles, walruses, pilot whales, and more. The park includes educational encounters with several of the larger animals to give viewers an opportunity to see how communication and hunting techniques of the animals.

The SeaWorld Rescue Team has been a part of over 40,000 animal rescues along the San Diego beaches and coastline. The teams at SeaWorld include zoological members who care for and rehabilitate these animals to return to the wild. A portion of every ticket price goes to their conservation and rescue efforts.

Fun Facts About SeaWorld San Diego

- There are festivals in the park year-round – Mardi Gras in the early spring, Electric Ocean in the summer, Halloween, and Christmas all offer special surprises.

- SeaWorld San Diego is home to some world-class roller coasters.

- The Electric Eel is a multi-launch coaster with twists and loops.

- Journey to Atlantic is a flume ride.

- Tidal Twister consists of dueling coasters with upside-down twists.

- Manta has two launches to get the feel of a darting manta ray.

- Emperor is a foot-dangling coaster with a 90 degree drop.

- Artic Rescue, new for 2023, contains icy thrills and speeds up to 40 mph (64.37 km/h).

- There is a Sesame Street Bay of Play for younger kids with character meet and greets.

Chapter 16

La Jolla Cove

La Jolla Cove is a small coastal inlet cove area with a beach (La Jolla Beach) surrounded by sandstone bluffs making for a beautiful area to spend the day. La Jolla Cove is in La Jolla which is a seaside community within San Diego. This area is one of the most photographed in southern California as you may see gulls, native plants, cormorants, and sea lions.

Cormorants are medium to large birds who are expert divers. In La Jolla, they will roost in the bluffs that are above the cove. Cormorants will weigh 0.77-11 pounds (0.35-5 kg) with a wingspan of 24-39 inches (60-100 cm). The birds are fish eaters and live along the coasts diving for their prey – sometimes as deep as 150 feet (45 m).

La Jolla Cove - Cormorants

Sea lions also dot the coastline in La Jolla Cove. The sea lions are seen mainly on the south bluff of La Jolla Cove, called Point La Jolla. The sea lions can be seen huddling together, barking at one another, playing in the water, or sometimes just sunbathing.

La Jolla Cove Sea Lions

Another great attraction at La Jolla Cove is the beach and the water sports available there. La Jolla Cove is a gateway to the San Diego-La Jolla Underwater Park, which is a protected, human-made marine reserve. Swimmers, divers, and snorkelers can explore this underwater park. Snorkelers and divers usually have visibility in the underwater park of up to 30 feet (9.14 m). Some other activities to try:

- Kayak tours

- Snorkel tours

- Snorkel and scuba rentals

Beach at La Jolla Cove

Fun Facts About La Jolla Cove

- La Jolla Cove is home to one of the oldest open ocean swims, the La Jolla Rough Water Swim. This event dates back to 1916.

- The water in La Jolla Cove is typically colder than anywhere else along the San Diego coast. This is because it faces into much colder, deeper water.

- It is one of the best spots to snorkel in the area because of the up to 30 ft (9.14 m) visibility - sometimes straight to the bottom.

Chapter 17

Birch Aquarium at Scripps

The Birch Aquarium at Scripps (or Birch Aquarium or Scripps Aquarium) is an aquarium in the La Jolla community of San Diego. The aquarium is the outreach center to the public for the Scripps Institute of Oceanography, which is a part of the University of California – San Diego. You can see the Scripps Institute and the Pacific Ocean from the aquarium.

The aquarium was established in 1903 when the Marine Biological Association of San Diego was established to conduct marine research in the Pacific Ocean. The Association was later renamed Scripps Institute of Oceanography in honor of supporters E.W. Scripps and Ellen Browning Scripps. The aquarium was created by the founders to show their discoveries to the world.

Exhibits at the Birch Aquarium at Scripps include:

- Beyster Family Little Blue Penguins – the only aquarium in the western U.S. to feature these small seabirds.

- Seadragons & Seahorses – see the 18 ft (5.5 m) wide, 9 ft (2.74 m) tall seadragon exhibit.

- Oddities – a comic book inspired exhibit that shows the superpowers of different ocean species.

- Hall of Fishes – a variety of marine life from the Pacific, heading from the Pacific Northwest down through the tropical Mexico waters.

- Research in Action: 100 Island Challenge – Located in the Hall of Fishes, it is a working laboratory serving as an experimental reef. This allows scientists to develop techniques to study coral and test equipment.

- Expedition at Sea: R/V Sally Ride Gallery – Dress like ocean studying scientists, learn from ship's crew recordings, and touch deep ocean artifacts on a research vessel at sea.

- Giant Kelp Forest – Explore an under-ocean forest in the 70,000-gallon (264,979-liter), 2-story giant kelp exhibit.

- Tide Pool Plaza – a hands-on exhibit with living tide pools. You will see sea stars, hermit crabs, sea cucumbers, sea anemones, and lobster.

Fun Facts About Birch Aquarium at Scripps

- If you are interested in knowing what it is like being a scientist, the aquarium offers times to interact with staff members, STEM events, and great summer camps.

- At the aquarium, you can meet the world's smallest penguins – the little blue penguins. The little blue penguins are less than 12 inches (30.48 cm) tall and weigh between 2 and 3 pounds (0.9 to 1.36 kg).

- The aquarium's rescued Loggerhead Sea Turtle makes its home in the Hall of Fishes.

Chapter 18

Torrey Pines State Natural Reserve

A 1,750-acre (708.2-hectare) coastal park, Torrey Pines State Natural Reserve is located in the La Jolla community of San Diego. A natural reserve is a special designation for an area that is home to threatened plants, animals, and habitats. There are 14 state natural reserves in California.

The reserve is dedicated to preserving the tree that it is named for, the Torrey Pine, and other wildlife that lives in this area. The Torrey Pine is a rare species of pine tree in California. The pine is a critically endangered species that grows only in the coastal areas of San Diego. There are close to 3,000 Torrey Pines in the reserve.

The Torrey Pine

In the reserve, there are 8 hiking trails. The most popular trails are:

- The Guy Fleming Trail – 0.7 mile (1,100 m) –the easiest trail in the reserve. It offers views of La Jolla.

- The Razor Point Trail – 1.4 miles (2,300 m) – a loop that provides a view of ravines and badlands and looks over the ocean.

- The Beach Trail – 0.75 mile (1,200 m) – a trail to the Torrey Pines State Beach.

Torrey Pines Natural Reserve

Fun Facts About the Torrey Pine and the Torrey Pines State Natural Reserve

- The Torrey Pine only grows naturally in two areas – San Diego and Santa Rosa Island – making it the rarest native pine tree in the United States.

- The Torrey Pines were originally called Soledad Pines (Solitary Pines) because they normally stand alone.

- The mule deer is the only type of deer in Southern California. This deer is seen in the reserve.

Chapter 19

San Diego Zoo Safari Park

The San Diego Zoo Safari Park is located in Escondido, California, just north of San Diego. It is an 1,800-acre (728.43-hectare) wildlife park. The park is home to over 3,600 animals of more than 300 different species. It is also an accredited botanical garden with more than 1.3 million plants. The safari park is home to many wild and endangered animals from Australia, South America, North America, Asia, Europe, and Africa. This park was built in 1964 to give the Asian and African animals more room to breed than the San Diego Zoo (its sister park in Balboa Park) could offer.

Quite a bit happens at the San Diego Zoo Safari Park. In addition to the very large Asian Savanna and African Plains exhibits, the park has facilities such as the Nikita Khan Rhino Rescue, libraries, large laboratory spaces, and a Frozen Zoo. The Rhino Rescue is working to help save the northern white rhino. The Frozen Zoo stores genetic material from animals (living cell cultures, sperm, embryos, and oocytes). The items are kept at very low temperatures (-321 °F (-196 °C)).

Elephants at the San Diego Zoo Safari Park

Some of the unique, amazing animals at the Safari Park are:

- Platypuses

- California Condors

- African Rhinos

- Bald Eagles

- Cheetahs

- Elephants

- Gorillas

- Tigers

Some of the great things to do and see at the Safari Park:

- Walkabout Australia – An animal encounter that provides a close up exhibit of kangaroos and wallabies. There is also a platypus exhibit in this area. The San Diego Safari Park has the only platypus exhibit that is not in Australia. In addition to these animals, you can also see freckled ducks, magpie geese, Australian brushturkeys, and radjah shelducks.

- Nairobi Village – Small animals are out with keepers at different times during the day. Some of the animals that you might see here are meerkats, ring-tail lemurs, Chilean flamingos, and white-fronted bee-eaters, among others.

- Petting Kraal – You have the opportunity to pet and groom goats in this interactive exhibit that is located inside Nairobi Village.

- Lagoon Loop – Feed the ducks here.

- Tiger Trail – Here you will see Sumatran tigers.

- African Plains and Asian Savanna – These areas cover over 300 acres (121.4 hectare) and are open range enclosures.

- Hidden Jungle – This is an indoor, climate-controlled exhibit featuring tropical birds and insects.

- Lion Camp – Here you can see African lions.

- Condor Ridge – Species in this area are the California condors, desert bighorn sheep, bald eagles, Harris hawks, burrowing owls, thick billed parrots, and desert tortoises.

The park also offers a variety of safaris for an additional fee.

Fun Facts About the San Diego Zoo Safari Park

- The safari park offers an African Tram. This free tram ride is a 25-minute tour of the Asian Savanna and the African Plains, giving a closer look at the animals.

- The safari park has played a big role in the recovery of the California condor. It brought the last 22 condors into captivity and started a captive breeding program. These were then released into the wild once again.

- One of the extra fee safaris includes a tethered balloon ride that helps visitors see the plains from 400 feet (120 m).

Chapter 20

San Diego Botanic Garden

The San Diego Botanic Garden is located in Encinitas, California, just north of San Diego. The garden covers 37 acres (15 hectares) and contains a number of unique gardens including bamboo groves, a subtropical fruit garden, a tropical rainforest, and some native California plants. The bamboo grove is of the largest bamboo collections known in the U.S.

The Botanic Garden has three children's gardens:

- Hamilton Children's Garden – This is the largest interactive garden for kids on the west coast of the U.S. and is very popular with older kids. Toni's Tree House is the most popular attraction in this garden, but there is also a labyrinth and a tic tac toe board. The tree house includes tunnels, rope bridges, and a spiral staircase.

In addition to the tree house and all of the other activities in this garden, there are other sections to explore: Incredible Edibles teaches about the herbs and plants that we eat, Garden Rhythms teaches about music you can make with instruments from nature like sticks, rocks, and water, a sketching area with coloring sheets, and a Spell & Smell garden filled with pots and plants labeled with letters of the alphabet.

- Seeds of Wonder – an interactive garden that is very popular with toddlers and young children. One of the top attractions at this garden is the model trains that make their way through miniatures in the garden. Another fun spot in this garden is the sandpit that is hiding plastic dinosaurs that kids can dig up. Older kids might enjoy transplanting succulents.

- Junior Quail Trail – This children's garden is an obstacle course. This course can be used by kids and adults to walk, jump, balance, and climb.

Some of the fascinating gardens are:

- The Bamboo Garden – rare bamboo groves not normally seen on the western coast of the U.S. There are more than 100 types of bamboo in the garden.

- Subtropical Fruit Garden – You will see the fruit naturally grown including banana trees.

- Undersea Succulent Garden – These are not small succulents; they look more like a coral reef.

Fun Facts About the San Diego Botanic Garden

- The Bamboo Garden contains the largest collection of bamboo in the United States.

- At Christmastime, the Botanic Garden transforms into the Botanic Wonderland with more than 100,000 lights.

- In the Bamboo Garden, there is a pond with lily pads, frogs, and turtles to see.

Chapter 21

The Carlsbad Flower Fields

The Carlsbad Flower Fields are located in the hills of North San Diego County. The flower fields are 55 acres (22.26 hectares) of Giant Tecolote Ranunculus flowers that bloom for about six to eight weeks per year, usually from early March through early May. The blooming of the flowers is a part of the local heritage of the area – an official welcome to spring in Southern California!

The Carlsbad Flower Fields

Fun Facts About the Carlsbad Flower Fields

- You can take a tractor-pulled wagon ride through the flower fields.

- There are 13 different colors of flowers planted at the flower gardens display with more than 700 million flowers blooming at peak bloom.

- The planting of the flowers starts as early as September.

Chapter 22

Cabrillo National Monument

The Cabrillo National Monument is located at the southernmost tip of the Point Loma Peninsula in San Diego. The National Monument is San Diego's only National Park and is set apart to commemorate the landing of Juan Rodriguez Cabrillo on September 28, 1542. Cabrillo's landing was the first time that a European explorer had set foot on the western coast of the United States. Cabrillo National Monument was set aside as a California Historical Landmark in 1932 and was then listed on the National Register of Historic Places in 1966.

Point Loma is a hilly peninsula (a piece of land that is connected to the mainland on one side but surrounded by water on the other sides). It is a community within the city of San Diego. Along with Coronado / Silver

Strand peninsula, the Point Loma peninsula defines the San Diego Bay and separates it from the Pacific Ocean. You can see the two peninsulas and the San Diego Bay in the map in this book. The term "Point Loma" is used to describe the entire peninsula as well as the neighborhoods of this area of San Diego. The original Spanish name of this peninsula was La Punta de Loma de San Diego, which is translated as Hill Point of San Diego. Most consider Point Loma as the starting point – the start of a new land!

The Point Loma Coast at Cabrillo National Monument

When visiting the National Monument, the best place to start is the Visitor Center. Here you will learn a little about the history of the park as well as have a chance to talk with park rangers. There is an auditorium showing several different films during the day. This is also the place to get your National Park Passport stamped!

At the Cabrillo National Monument is San Diego's first lighthouse, the Old Point Loma Lighthouse. The lighthouse's construction was started in 1854 and was completed in 1855. The lamp of the lighthouse was first lit on November 15, 1855. The lighthouse was built on the highest location on the point. It didn't take long to realize that the elevation would be a problem as the light was covered in fog and clouds quite a lot of the time. So, a new lighthouse was built and opened at a lower elevation in 1891.

At that point, the old lighthouse was boarded up and abandoned. It was even recommended that the lighthouse be destroyed, but because of the great views from the tower, it was popular with visitors.

The Old Point Loma Lighthouse

There is a sandstone statue of Juan Rodriguez Cabrillo at the National Monument. It stands 14 ft (4.3 m) tall and weighs in at 14,000 pounds (6,400 kg). The sculpture was sculpted by Alvaro de Bree. The statue that is at the National Monument was commissioned in 1939 by the Portuguese government to be given to the United States. Interestingly, it was originally going to the Golden Gate International Exposition in California, but it arrived too late to be displayed. The statue was placed in storage in California unto 1940 when Senator Ed Fletcher helped to get the statue sent to San Diego. It was stored in San Diego for a while and then placed at the Cabrillo National Monument in 1949.

Juan Rodríguez Cabrillo Sculpture

Fun Facts About the Cabrillo National Monument

- In the winter, Cabrillo National Monument is a great place to watch grey whales migrate from the Artic on their way to Mexico.

- Cabrillo was known as the "Columbus of San Diego."

- The original sandstone statue of Cabrillo suffered weathering and was replaced with a limestone replica in 1988.

Chapter 23

Whale Watching in San Diego

Whale watching in San Diego is a year-round activity. In San Diego, you can whale watch up-close on the water as well as from the shore in various places. The 70 miles of coastline and the fact that San Diego is along the migration path of several whale species makes it one of the best places to whale watch in all of California.

View of a Whale Watching Tour in San Diego

Gray Whale Watching

During the winter and spring (mid-December-April), more than 20,000 gray whales make the round-trip journey from Alaska to calving grounds in the warm lagoons of Mexico. After giving birth and allowing their young to grow strong, the whales journey travel back north in the spring. The gray whales travel close to the coastline and can be seen from the shore. Gray whales can grow to close to 50 ft (15.24 m) in length.

Blue Whale Watching

During the summer and fall (mid-June-September) the largest creatures on earth – the blue whales – can be found off the coast of San Diego. Large groups of blue whales (sometimes 2,000-3,000) feed off the coast during the summer months. Blue whales can grow to 100 ft (30.48 m) in length. The blue whales feed farther off the coast so the best way to see them is by boat.

Humpback and Fin Whale Watching

Humpback Whales and Fin Whales can be seen off the coast of San Diego throughout the year.

Whale Watching from Shore

Some recommended places to spot the gray whale migration from the shore are the Cabrillo National Monument, the Torrey Pines State Reserve, and Birch Aquarium at Scripps. There are hiking trails in all of these locations that offer views of the Pacific Ocean.

Whale Watching Tours

A whale watching tour on the water is one of the best ways to view whales. You are in a small boat that gets you close to the water level. Tour guides are excellent at choosing the best places to view whales. Here are a few whale watching tours available in San Diego:

- San Diego Whale Watch – Offering whale watching tours year-round with a naturalist available on every tour. The tours leave from Mission Bay and are between 2 and 3 hours in length.

- Next Level Sailing – This tour leaves from Shelter Island with tours lasting between 3.5 and

4 hours. Tours are offered year-round on the 139 ft (42.37 m) Yacht America.

- Flagship Cruises & Events – Leaving from downtown San Diego, this company offers twice daily whale watching tours during the gray whale migration. The Birch Aquarium at Scripps provides naturalists on these tours to add more insight.

Fun Facts About Whales

- Blue whales are the largest animals that have lived on earth.

- Gray whales can travel more than 14,000-mile (2,253-km) round trip on their migration to give birth.

- Whales communicate with one another using sound.

Chapter 24

Walking Tours

The areas in and around San Diego offer big opportunities for walking tours – Balboa Park, Coronado, La Jolla, Liberty Station (on Point Loma), and Old Town. Spending a little time out and about with an interesting tour guide may be just what you need to learn a little more about this area's history!

Here are a few of the tour companies in the area and some of what they offer:

San Diego Walks

These tours take you off the beaten path! Some of their tour offerings are: The Secrets and Highlights of Balboa Park – get a full overview of the park and its history, Old Town Tales – sampling the best of Old Town, Liberty Station – explore the area and the naval base, and Coronado History and Highlights – from multi-million-dollar homes to the sandy beaches along the Pacific.

Another Side of San Diego Tours

These walking tours explore the fascinating history of the area. The tours offered by this company are: The Coronado Walking Tour – visit the Hotel Del Coronado and see the Coronado Bridge, The Old Town Walking Tour – explore the history of San Diego in the birthplace of San Diego, The Balboa Park Walking Tour – stroll through the park learning the history and enjoying the gardens, The Little Italy Walking Tour – the best shopping in San Diego and home to some of the best food too, The La Jolla Walking Tour – walk along the coastal bluffs, caves, and shorelines before journeying to Prospect and Girad Ave., The San Diego Tide Pool Tour – see the marine ecosystem up-close!

So Diego Explore + Experience

These tours help you explore the local scene – Never Basic, Always Adventurous! This group loves all things San Diego. As a group of professional tour guides and event planners, their tours revolve around local establishments to create great experiences! They include tours of Little Italy, Old City, and the Gaslamp Quarter, visiting restaurants, dessert shops, and cool hole-in-the-wall stops.

Chapter 25

Bike and Kayak Tours

Biking is a great way to explore downtown San Diego or the neighborhoods of La Jolla, Mission Bay, or Coronado in more depth. If getting on the water is more to your liking, there are a variety of kayak tours available too! The following companies may have just the tour you are looking for.

Bike and Kayak Tours – La Jolla and Coronado

This company offers a kayak tour of sea caves in the La Jolla area – 7 caves in total. The company also offers a leopard shark encounter snorkeling adventure. The kayak tour is offered year-round, every hour starting at 9 am, and the tour lasts about 2 hours. The snorkeling tour is offered during the summer months (June-September) and lasts about an hour. At times, Bike and Kayak Tours offers a La Jolla bike tour.

Cave Kayaking in La Jolla

Scenic Cycle Tours

Scenic Cycle Tours offers scenic rides through Coronado and Mission Bay. The Mission Bay tour offers a ride along the boardwalk, Mission Beach, Belmont Park, and the roller coaster. The Coronado tour includes the Hotel del Coronado, riding along bike paths, and a view of the Coronado Bridge.

Biking in Mission Bay

I hope you enjoyed your trip to San Diego! Next, let's head east to visit the historical US city of Boston Massachusetts where we will learn about a 2.5-mile (4-kilometer) trail that marks many locations important to the American Revolution!

kid-friendly-family-vacations.com/booktour-boston

————————————————————————————

Are you ready to visit Asia? Let's visit Seoul South Korea where you will explore Royal Palaces and learn about the unique street food!

kid-friendly-family-vacations.com/booktour-seoul

————————————————————————————

Signup for my newsletter for all upcoming book updates as well as some cool San Diego puzzles and coloring pages!

kid-friendly-family-vacations.com/sdfun

————————————————————————————

Visit all the cities in the Hey Kids! Let's Visit series...

kid-friendly-family-vacations.com/series

————————————————————————————

If you enjoyed your visit to San Diego, please leave a review to help others also learn more about San Diego whether traveling or learning from home.

kid-friendly-family-vacations.com/review-sd

Also By Teresa Mills and Kid Friendly Family Vacations

Hey Kids! Let's Visit Washington DC
Hey Kids! Let's Visit A Cruise Ship
Hey Kids! Let's Visit New York City
Hey Kids! Let's Visit London England
Hey Kids! Let's Visit San Francisco
Hey Kids! Let's Visit Savannah Georgia
Hey Kids! Let's Visit Paris France
Hey Kids! Let's Visit Charleston South Carolina
Hey Kids! Let's Visit Chicago
Hey Kids! Let's Visit Rome Italy
Hey Kids! Let's Visit Boston
Hey Kids! Let's Visit Philadelphia
Hey Kids! Let's Visit San Diego
Hey Kids! Let's Visit Seattle
Hey Kids! Let's Visit Seoul South Korea

More from Kid Friendly Family Vacations

BOOKS

Books to help build your kids / grandkids life experiences through travel and learning
https://kid-friendly-family-vacations.com/books

COLORING AND ACTIVITY PAGKAGES

Coloring pages, activity books, printable travel journals, and more in our Etsy shop
https://kid-friendly-family-vacations.com/etsy

RESOURCES FOR TEACHERS

Resources for teachers on Teachers Pay Teachers
https://kid-friendly-family-vacations.com/tpt

It is our mission to help you build your children's and grand-children's life experiences through travel. Not just traveling with your kids... building their Life Experiences"! Join our community here:
https://kid-friendly-family-vacations.com/join

Acknowledgements

Proofreading / Editing

Katie Erickson – https://www.katieericksonediting.com

Cover Photos

Belmont Park - © f8grapher / depositphotos.com

Maritime Museum of San Diego - Star of India - © sainaniritu / depositphotos.com

Torrey Pine Tree - © Cavan / depositphotos.com

San Diego Zoo - sea seal - © Wirestock / depositphotos.com

La Jolla Cove – beach - © Jfortner2015 / depositphotos.com

Photos in Book

USS Midway Museum – Flight Deck - © f8grapher / depositphotos.com

USS Midway Museum – USS Midway - © rigucci / depositphotos.com

Maritime Museum of San Diego - Star of India - © sainaniritu / depositphotos.com

SeaWorld San Diego - © pngstudio / depositphotos.com

La Jolla – cormorants - © Devon / depositphotos.com

La Jolla Cove - sea lions - © czuber / depositphotos.com

La Jolla Cove – beach - © Jfortner2015 / depositphotos.com

Torrey Pines State Natural Reserve - © weissdergeier / depositphotos.com

Torrey Pine Tree - © Cavan / depositphotos.com

Zoo Safari Park – Elephants - © maryprentice / depositphotos.com

Carlsbad Flower Fields - © bonandbon / depositphotos.com

Cabrillo National Monument - © demerzel21 / depositphotos.com

Point Loma - © rruntsch / depositphotos.com

Old Point Loma Lighthouse - © sprokop / depositphotos.com

Whale Watching in San Diego - © ronniechua / depositphotos.com

Cave Kayak - La Jolla - © stephstarr9363@gmail.com / depositphotos.com

Biking in Mission Bay - © bonandbon / depositphotos.com

About the Author

Teresa Mills is the bestselling author of the "Hey Kids! Let's Visit..." Book Series for Kids! Teresa's goal through her books and website is to help parents / grandparents who want to build the life experiences of their children / grandchildren through travel and learning activities.

She is an active mother and Mimi. She and her family love traveling in the USA, and internationally too! They love exploring new places, eating cool foods, and having yet another adventure as a family! With the Mills, it's all about traveling as family.

In addition to traveling, Teresa enjoys reading, hiking, biking, and helping others.

Join in the fun at

kid-friendly-family-vacations.com

Made in United States
Orlando, FL
25 February 2024

44075950R00068